Secrets We Don't Keep

By: Dr. Shareeda Tyaire

Copyright © 2020 by Shareeda Tyaire

All rights reserved. This book or any portion thereof may not be reproduced or used in any manner whatsoever without the express written permission of the author and/or publisher except for the use of brief quotations in a book review.

Illustrator: Kat Powell

Publisher: Bruised and Unbroken

ISBN: 978-1-7350368-8-5

I dedicate this one to my husband, my protector, Priest Tyaire.

Thank you for reassuring me that I am now safe.

There are
good secrets

AND THERE ARE BAD SECRETS.

OR WHEN YOU DON'T TELL SOMEONE ABOUT A GIFT YOU GOT THEM FOR A SPECIAL OCCASION.

YOU DON'T TELL, BECAUSE YOU WANT THEM TO BE SURPRISED.

Bad secrets are when you don't tell anybody that someone

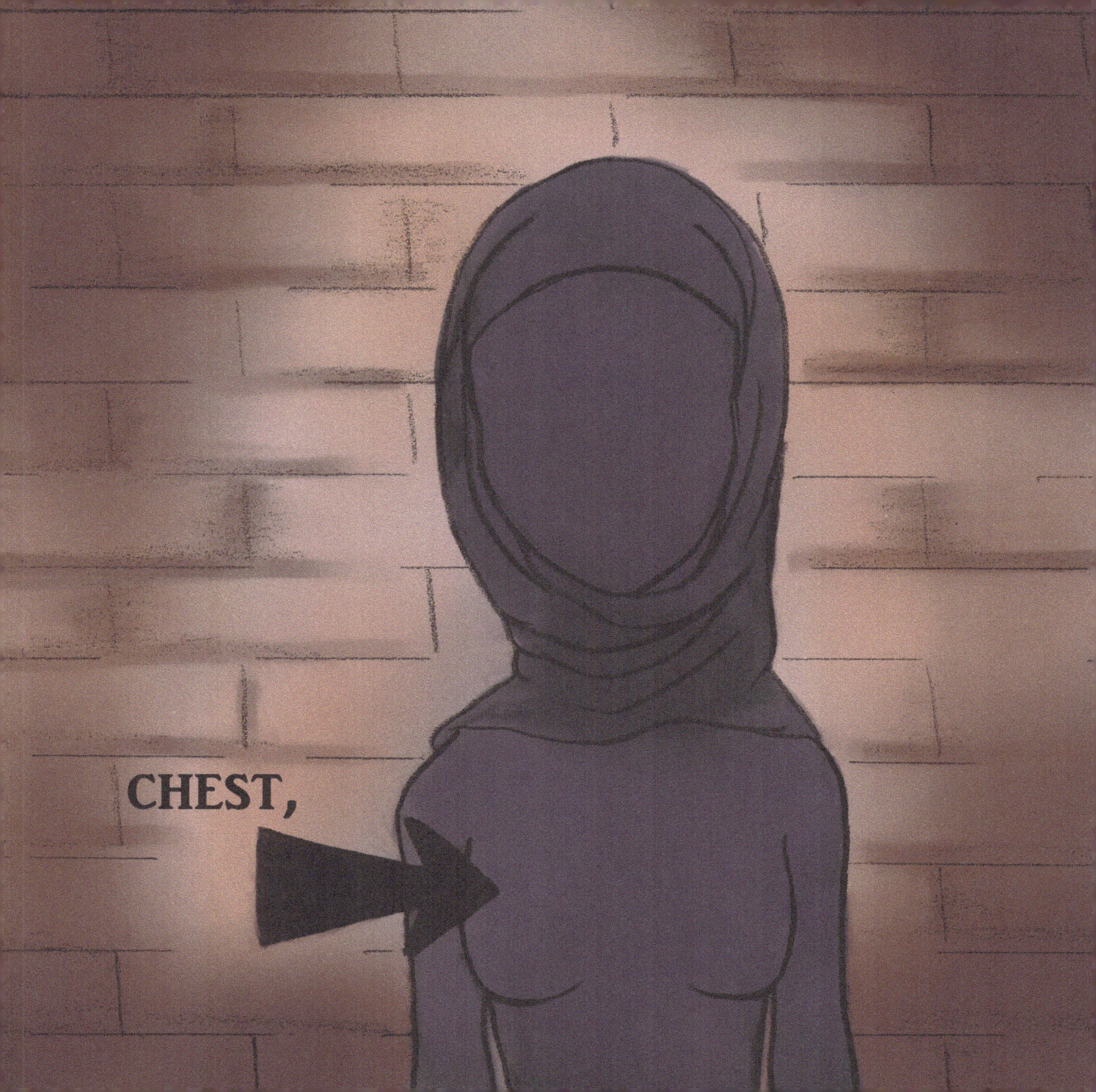

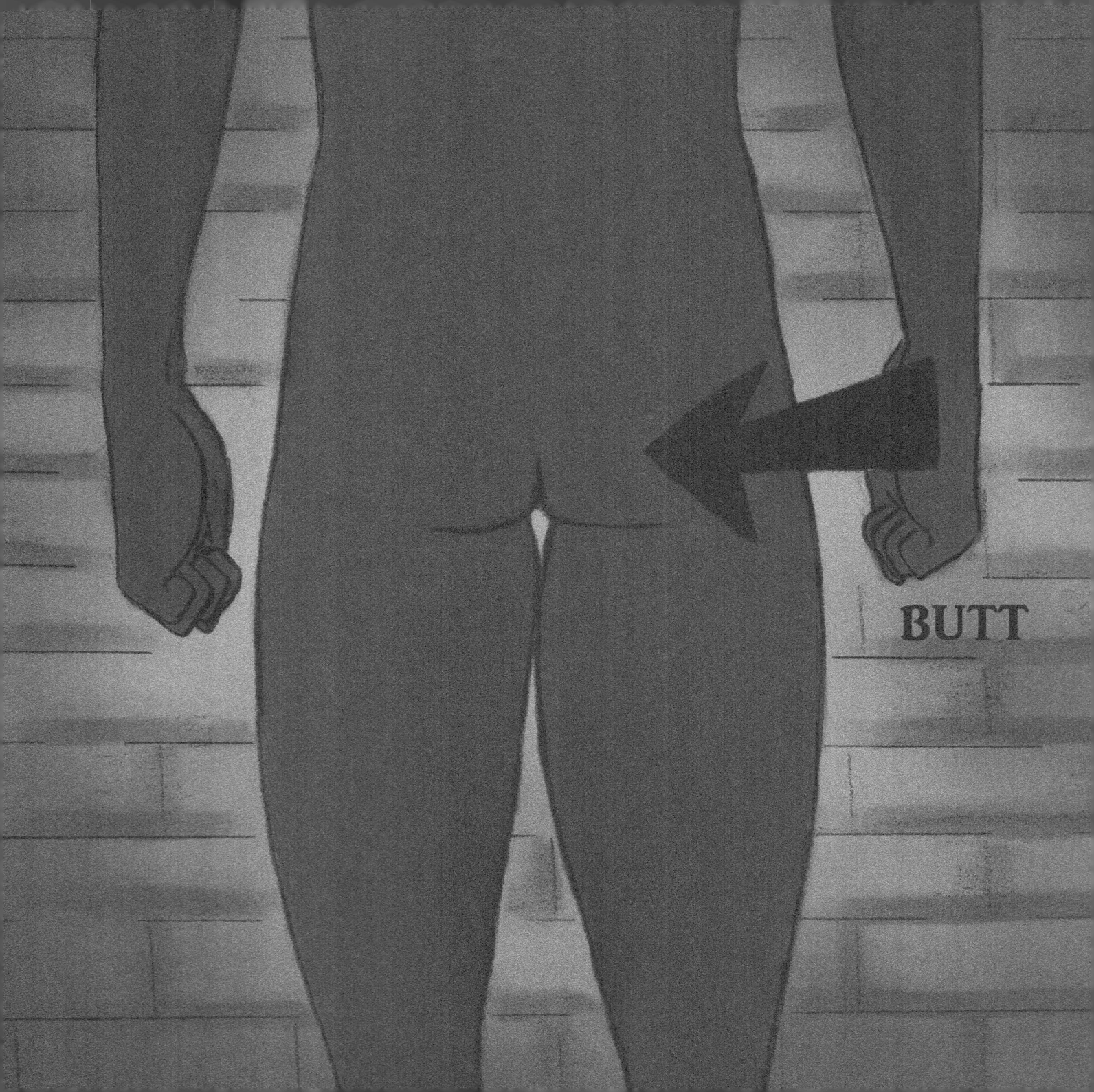

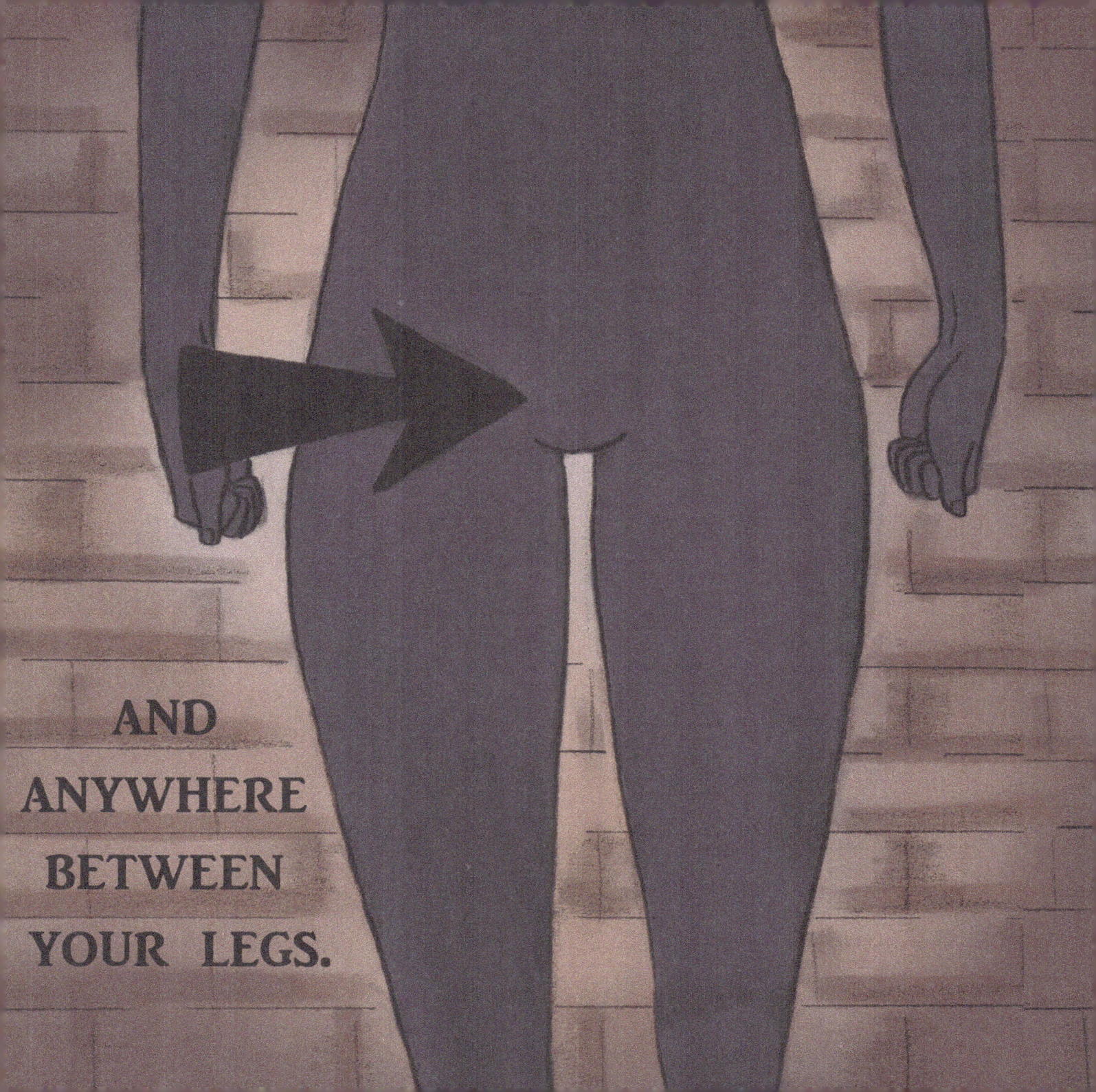

Some families use different words to describe private parts.

IF ANYBODY TELLS YOU TO KEEP A SECRET THAT HURTS YOU, MAKES YOU FEEL SAD, OR MAKES YOU SCARED;

Even if they tell you that they will hurt you or your family if you tell the secret,

The End